KEEPING A PUFFER AFLOAT

VIC 56 crew at the Queen's Diamond Jubilee Pageant 2012. From left – Bob and Julie Cooper, Mike and Roz Willis, Tom Young, Rupert, James, Amy and Suzette Lodge, Liz, Henry and Catherine Cleary and Richard Beet (Richard Beet)

KEEPING A PUFFER AFLOAT

THE STORY OF A SMALL STEAMSHIP

Henry Cleary

Copyright © 2023 Henry Cleary

The moral right of the author has been asserted.

Apart from any fair dealing for the purposes of research or private study, or criticism or review, as permitted under the Copyright, Designs and Patents Act 1988, this publication may only be reproduced, stored or transmitted, in any form or by any means, with the prior permission in writing of the publishers, or in the case of reprographic reproduction in accordance with the terms of licences issued by the Copyright Licensing Agency. Enquiries concerning reproduction outside those terms should be sent to the publishers.

Matador
Unit E2 Airfield Business Park,
Harrison Road, Market Harborough,
Leicestershire. LE16 7UL
Tel: 0116 2792299
Email: books@troubador.co.uk
Web: www.troubador.co.uk/matador
Twitter: @matadorbooks

ISBN 978 1803137 513

British Library Cataloguing in Publication Data.
A catalogue record for this book is available from the British Library.

Printed and bound in Great Britain by 4edge Limited
Typeset in 12pt Minion Pro by Troubador Publishing Ltd, Leicester, UK

Matador is an imprint of Troubador Publishing Ltd

To the crews of VIC 56
and the Port Auxiliary Service
at HM Naval Base, Rosyth

VIC 51 in the Scheldt supporting the advance to Antwerp in 1945 (William Dieleman)

ACKNOWLEDGEMENTS

Keeping VIC 56 going has been a social enterprise and a great many people have helped in some way. Many of those are mentioned in Note 2 and many unnamed others also deserve credit. Thanks in particular to those who contributed memories as included in this text and in particular photographers Richard Beet and the late Alan Jenner, professional Thames skippers, and Bob Gwynne, transport historian of York. As will be clear in Chapter 3, my wife, Liz, and family demonstrated the greatest loyalty and resilience whatever events a VIC voyage might bring. To all I record my deep thanks. To any I may have inadvertently missed, my equal thanks.

Cover illustration: VIC 56 in Sea Reach (Alan Jenner).

ABOUT THE AUTHOR

Henry Cleary was born in the City of Derry, Northern Ireland, in 1951. He joined the Department of Environment, London, in 1977 and retired as Deputy Director, Growth Programmes, in 2011. He is currently Chair of the Maritime Heritage Trust. He and his wife live in Herne Hill, South London.

INTRODUCTION – WHY?

Why take on 150 tonnes of slowly rusting steel and try to keep it going? In the 1960s, as it appeared to an enthusiast, heritage was disregarded; there were the Beeching railway closures, the end of steam on BR, ready destruction of buildings, records and other cultural vandalism in pursuit of modernisation and the economic growth of post war Britain. Fortunately a *Titfield Thunderbolt* style grass roots movement of volunteers had started rescuing things and showing that lovely and characterful machines could be saved even if they didn't fit a commercial niche. As has been observed, this generation of preservationists were fanatics – they had to be.

Sadly hardly any of this reached the maritime sector. Until HRH Prince Philip forced officialdom to take ship preservation seriously with the saving of the Cutty Sark, and his support for a collection of over 20 historic vessels rescued by the Maritime Trust in the 1970s, the whole idea of ship preservation was dismissed as too difficult and likely to end in failure. Since the 1990s some help for public projects has come via the National Lottery Heritage Fund, although most of this has been for static maritime museum vessels. As ever the main burden of vessel preservation continues to fall on individuals and their supporters, learning on the job and cajoling help and contributions wherever they can.

In September 1978 I joined the movement by submitting a bid (for a little over the scrap price) to the Ministry of Defence (Navy) to acquire *VIC 56*, a naval puffer - a small cargo vessel used to carry ammunition and all types of stores - laid up since 1975 at Rosyth on the Firth of Forth. VICs were part of the wartime building programme, to a design based on the famous Clyde puffer, and used as a supply vessel in naval bases around Britain and all over the world.

VIC 56 itself is a humble craft but is special because she is one of only a tiny number of working steamers to survive (including one other large VIC) and is a credit to the craftsmen builders at Faversham (James Pollock and Sons) who created her. Marine steam today means the steam turbines in nuclear submarines and gas tankers with only a handful of sea-going UK heritage steamers.

> **Naval lifestory** For most of her career the 1945 built *VIC 56* led a pretty routine existence as a Naval Armaments Vessel in Scotland running up and down the Firth of Forth between warships at Rosyth and the munitions stores at Crombie and at Bandeath (near Stirling), with occasional mishaps and excitements. Her most interesting task (April 1961) was to carry stores, a jeep

Introduction – why?

and a sectioned hut to the then uninhabited island of South Rona in the Inner Hebrides (between Skye, Raasay and the mainland). *VIC 56* sailed via the Caledonian Canal and loaded more stores and naval personnel on the west coast. Despite a rocky ledge berth, *VIC 56* got its load ashore as planned and this expedition was a forerunner of establishing the British Underwater Testing and Evaluation Centre (BUTEC) on Rona, now run by QinetiQ. There were plenty of *Parahandy* style adventures en route and a couple of unofficial teenage crew seemed to have wangled a passage.

VIC 56 in 1978 in Rosyth Dockyard alongside the Harbour Training frigates Duncan and Eastbourne (Henry Cleary)

Over 40 years of preservation VIC 56 has been steamed and sailed under its own power each year and reached places as exotic as Vlissingen on the Scheldt in Holland as well as many small creeks and corners of the Thames Estuary.

Hundreds of people have helped to keep her going in some way and this account can only give a selective impression of what was involved. Self-taught has often been the way for crew of coastal craft and this includes the pre WW2 steam "shovel" engineers around the Irish Sea and British coasts, including the Thames Estuary, who have been an inspiration.

In 2019 with the ageing of the volunteer team, another change of owner was required. After a search, *VIC 56* was gifted by me to Portsmouth Naval Base Property Trust (PNBPT) where, thanks to their support and the good work of the Boathouse 4 volunteers, she can be seen (and is occasionally in steam) as part of the unique PNBPT national collection of naval support craft.

Active preservation, displaying and keeping going large machines can be seen as an arts project and needs to be re-interpreted afresh by successive generations who will each see something different. There is no certain route to success; this account sets out our experience in case it is of interest to others. What will work for new people? Online media can do a lot to promote heritage but it cannot recreate the heat, smell, motion and rhythm of cranks of a working steamer's engine or its quiet, upright, stately passage through coastal waters. Let us hope that something of that survives.

Introduction – why?

Leaving Rosyth in 1979 (John Allen)

Skipper Chris Harris in wheelhouse. Makeshift azimuth ring (curtain rail and hand mirror) which enabled bearings to be taken can just be seen on compass (Henry Cleary)

Chapter 1

GO OR NO GO

At around 1500 on the 14th April 1979, an Easter Saturday, an elderly, rusty, small steamship dropped anchor in Dunbar Roads and the crew of 5 debated whether to continue on a voyage south into preservation or return to Granton, Edinburgh from where they had set out 8 hours earlier with a borderline weather forecast. It was 6 months since acceptance by MoD of the purchase bid and the goodwill of the authorities at Rosyth had allowed the formal "one month to remove your vessel" to stretch but I sensed that our limit had now been reached.

As with any voyage there were worries – uncertain weather, people availability (for all concerned this was in spare time), supplies and which harbours would offer a berth on what was intended to be part one of a 400 mile voyage to London. We had sustained morale by getting advice from old hands in Rosyth but now the moment had come. The vessel hadn't been to sea for 5 years, barely had the basics for navigation, and none of the 5 crew: an experienced yachtsman, Peter Erskine; me - a civil servant steam enthusiast; my younger brother Julian; the late John Allen, a post-grad biologist; and Chris Harris, now a civil servant, but also a retired Royal Navy officer (Engineer), had been to sea on it previously. That morning it had been agreed to sail only on a provisional basis – being prepared to go back if necessary.

Sailing along the Scottish coast, the anchor and windlass were tried out for the first time and one of the anchor cables ranged on deck and marked to indicate depth – exhausting work. The primitive VHF radio had proved successful at least on the local channels; it was the only modern communication on board. There was no echo sounder, only a lead line and the compass had lacked any means of taking a bearing. Here John Allen came to the rescue by fashioning a crude azimuth ring from brass curtain rail and a piece of hand mirror. It proved highly effective and underway the deviation of the compass was calibrated and bearings taken. It helped also that the vessel was then an oil burner – not without its challenges - but much less effort than if it had been coal burning (to which she was later converted).

Visits to Rosyth between purchase and sailing had not been wasted. Teams from the preserved steam vessels *Kerne* and *VIC 32* had come for a couple of weekends to lead the process of dismantling and checking the boiler mountings, doors, valves and working weekends with other friends followed. A really helpful boiler inspector, Roger Pedrick, carried out a survey and helped remedy some of the

Steaming south – two crew on deck (Henry Cleary)

minor defects found. Former VIC crew from other Port Auxiliary Service vessels and other Dockyard staff called in to provide help in various forms, answer questions and advise, in particular the former VIC engineer Dick Drury and Chief Petty Officer Bill McLelland, a Chief Petty Officer RN Training Instructor, who later came on part of the voyage south.

A large group of supporters - friends and relatives - had been recruited, many persuaded to make loans as the original budget (a bank loan as the Manager viewed the occupation of civil servant as low risk!) had been overrun some time previously with the cost of life-saving gear, supplies etc; and of the 2 liferafts, one was borrowed and the other on hire purchase.

But now we were out at sea, on our own and the vote was to continue south. The weather forecast had improved but crucial also was the decision of our naval officer to accept command of the venture, with the support of Peter, leaving the engine room to me and we agreed to work watches through the night, relying on our oil lamps and Tilley lamps and tinned meals from the oil burning galley. Around 35 hours after leaving Granton we berthed in Sunderland at 17.35 on Easter Sunday. After a rest, and a further passage of 12 hours, we reached Whitby and then, after another 25 hours steaming, Grimsby, Alexandra Dock on 19th April 1979. Challenges continued, such as getting into Whitby despite Chris, the skipper, being told that we needed twice our speed to be able to cross the tidal streams running across the harbour entrance.

Ranging and marking the anchor cable off Bass Rock (John Allen)

Interior of focsle – berths for 3 seamen and 1 stoker (Henry Cleary)

The compound steam engine (Richard Beet)

Off the Lincolnshire coast, slogging through a hostile tide and wind the VIC's progress dwindled and after a long night came to anchor in the Wash, some of the exhausted crew stretched out on the hold in the sunshine to recover. The Wash ports proved to be much less accommodating than in the north, fearing no doubt that a rusting antique could be a liability. We were rescued from this by the helpful Harbourmaster at Wells next the Sea who not only offered a berth but took pride in coming out and piloting the vessel onto the Wells quayside. But by now the crew were 3 days late back in their offices. Scouring Wells for a taxi to make the last train to London from Norwich, the adventure was not over. Half way to Norwich the taxi had a puncture but after a pit stop tyre change and a race to the station, the train was just caught as the guard was blowing his whistle.

Go or no go

At anchor in the Wash - exhausted crew (Henry Cleary)

By this time leave was in very short supply but more friends (and relatives) signed up for further stages of the voyage and by using weekends Rotherhithe on the Thames was reached on 10th June. At this time the Thames Barrier was still under construction, radio permission was strictly required to transit and now the primitive crystal based VHF failed on the job. The situation was saved by hailing an overtaking tanker barge through a rolled up navigation chart and following him through the works; an early introduction to practical help on the river.

A post trip scene at Rotherhithe in 1979. New Caledonian wharf next door was still handling cargo (Henry Cleary)

VIC 56 in a short lived red hull colour moored on Greenland Pier, Surrey Docks c1980 (Henry Cleary)

Chapter 2

LIFE ON THE RIVER

On the 29th July 1981 much of the nation's attention was focused on Westminster Abbey but *VIC 56* was steaming down the river from Greenland Pier, Surrey Docks, its usual berth at that time, to the Port of London Authority Moorings Depot at the entrance to the King George V Dock, also strangely working that day. The PLA had kindly agreed to lift out, without charge, four 5 tonne concrete blocks from the VIC hold. These had been provided in Rosyth to help ballast the vessel on the voyage south. It was typical of the sympathetic seafarer response the vessel often got. While under way the usually very proper Woolwich VHF radio (the station for Thames navigation) briefly broadcast Charles and Di's wedding vows.

PLA lifting out the concrete blocks on Royal Wedding Day 1981 (Henry Cleary)

In the late 1970s much of the former Docks area of south and east London was fairly derelict and empty following the closures due to containerisation so it had not been too difficult to find a berth for *VIC 56*. This was with an embryonic sailing club (mainly boat-builders) renting, from Southwark Council, a corner of hard standing close to the entrance to the Greenland Dock. There was also a damaged wooden pier, almost severed when a ship had ploughed into it.

This was not a place to show off old vessels but it was a fairly sheltered location and, with very little housing, could tolerate the noise of work on board, and there were a few people around to help keep an eye on things. At this point the river was almost fresh water, a big advantage in slowing corrosion on a steel hull, and the berth had a chalk campshed to provide a softer bottom and an excellent base from which to work on the hull at low tide.

Keeping ahead of the property investors Old boats and new property investment are rarely a good mix. By 1984 Greenland Dock was being redeveloped and *VIC 56* had to find a new berth, in this case just upstream at the Trinity Business Centre, a small business development by Bermondsey boy Tommy Steele, but managed by a former deep sea mariner, John Taylor, who was sympathetic and really helpful. In 1997 this too succumbed to the Docklands housing redevelopment boom and, after more searching, cycling along the riverbank and with help from David Little of the London Docklands Development Corporation, another berth was found at Trinity Buoy Wharf where the River Lea enters the Thames. This former Trinity House Depot was embarking on a new career as an arts venue and workshop space led by Eric Reynolds and was a sympathetic, historic location. Over time the VIC proved a good platform from which to observe successive plans to revive the East Thames Corridor/Gateway (on which I had worked as a day job) and in 2003 John Prescott, then Deputy Prime Minister, a strong supporter of reviving Britain's merchant fleet, came down river on VIC 56 to view it, transferring at Greenhithe to the PLA for a visit to their latest operations centre.

The second berth at Rotherhithe – Trinity Business Centre (Henry Cleary)

The Rotherhithe berths linked well into the river community. River people could see what we were trying to do and were sympathetic. The river police were always friendly, often came alongside and on one occasion found and returned the ship's boat which had worn through its mooring line and wandered during the night.

The berth also served for living on board (which was part of the "financial" plan) though conditions were basic, with no electric or water supply. The coal stove in the after-cabin could be banked (if you were lucky) to stay alight all day but not plus an evening. The only quick warmth to be had returning late was to light a Tilley lamp. The river provided the delight of watching the dawn, the seasons, and wildlife as well as passing traffic but it couldn't be switched off – reading or sleeping, the ear was always attuned for the mooring lines taking up and the movements caused by large vessels (and on a very rare occasion, a rope breaking). After 2 years the attractions of a developing relationship ashore, easy access to a bath and the opportunity to read in silence won out, but all the loans from the voyage south had been repaid and every corner of the vessel thoroughly investigated.

The great challenge with any old vessel is how to maintain it, prevent it looking a wreck and at least slow the processes of rust and decay. In 1979 there was no National Lottery heritage Fund and virtually no grants. As Nick Walker of *VIC 32* said, you had to reckon on paying for work or doing it yourself, treating any help from friends or enthusiasts as a bonus. Compared with a similar commercial vessel, *VIC 56* had been well maintained at Rosyth but the climate there was harsh. She had been laid up for 5 years and before that had less attention as her service life ended. Quarter inch thick chunks of rust were not rare, particularly around the hold coaming, under the stern and around the ballast tank which had water on both sides, but the original interiors still looked good.

The prospect was daunting. I found that morale can be boosted by getting a small section looking good, and then to think small, not big; focussing on what can be done in a 2 hour session, then ensuring you do a certain number of these each month, then standing back each year. Most areas were on a 5 year cycle – yes, it all has to be done time and again. Reaching the recesses and the hold requires an obsessional commitment but after a week in the office, the chipping could become therapeutic at times and the thought of 2 hours sitting on a painting stage over the side with a chipping hammer pretty attractive on a nice summer day.

Deck ready for chipping and painting – a never ending task
(Henry Cleary)

On painting stage – a nice job (Henry Cleary)

A good volunteer job at Rotherhithe – Dave Morphew, the VIC's first Chief Engineer: "When first acquired the VIC was fitted with a derrick consisting of a steel boom, some 30ft long, pivoted off the mast and long enough to reach the other end of the hold - just in front of the wheelhouse - where it sat on a steel bracket. The boom was heavy; the only way to lift it was to use the winch which, of course, required the boiler to be in steam. A shorter, lighter weight, boom would be far more practical and allow manual operation, enabling material to be loaded and the rowing boat to be lowered over the side. Tony and Alan of the Rotherhithe Sailing Club kindly donated an unused mast for this purpose but first the steel boom had to be removed, but without raising steam! At the time I was driving a Land Rover so it was decided this would be used to provide the lifting force; a pulley block was shackled to the top of the mast and a line run from the end of the boom, through the block, to the tow hitch on the Land Rover on the dock alongside. In case the whole exercise went wrong a number of old pallets (retained for fire lighting) were arranged under the boom to act as a 'crash barrier'. Everything went to plan. The free end of the boom was lifted clear of its rest, then lowered on to the hold hatch covers; the line was then attached to the 'fixed' end of the boom and, having removed the lock nut, it was lifted clear of the pivot (with some 'persuasion' from a large hammer!) and lowered to the covers. Job done! The old boom could now be cut up, with the hinge pivot being retained for use on the light weight version."

Life on the river

Removing the steel derrick with Dave Morphew (Henry Cleary)

Lots of mistakes were made in the early years – not understanding different paints and their compatibility, or the benefit of using an air gun for descaling etc, but gradually the work got more effective, though it was only on rare occasions (eg the Queen's Diamond Jubilee Pageant, 2012) that all of the VIC looked good. But then people decided that worn equalled authentic; most heart-warming was an Open Day where the young people attending passed by the other highly polished attendee vessels and headed for the careworn rusty survivor saying "We want to see the really old one".

The mainly gentle life on the river was coming to an end. Trinity Buoy Wharf, though a sympathetic base, was a difficult, highly exposed drying berth. As river use intensified, particularly with fast ferries, RIBs and patrol craft, the damage caused by wash to the ship's bottom proved costly and unacceptable and in 2005 the VIC was accepted for a berth at Chatham Historic Dockyard.

Chapter 3

STEERING FROM THE GALLEY

How to attract people to help run the VIC? In 1970 a former Lord Provost of Edinburgh had established the Land, Sea and Air Youth Club in memory of his son, Malcolm Miller, with a small Vic (renamed "*Auld Reekie*"). She was a charter vessel with 2 crew to take youth parties from deprived areas on expeditions into the Highlands and Islands. Unfortunately the youth tended to exploit the opportunities of the trip for further wayward activity so that by the mid-1970s the charity was happy to take less challenging groups such as students. In each of 2 summers I organised a one week trip with a mixed group of 10-12 and it worked very well – a great introduction to puffers.

A holiday weekend on VIC 32 in the Thames Estuary in 1978 (Henry Cleary)

A shorter but similar trip was organised with Nick Walker who was converting *VIC 32* in St Katharine's Dock, London for a her new career offering holidays in the Highlands (which she still does) and welcomed volunteers. These ventures showed that you didn't need to be an enthusiast to enjoy a day on a puffer as long as there was a good mix of people and a continuous supply of tea and cake. That principle was key to getting *VIC 56* going after coming to London. Friends from work and university welcomed doing something a bit different on their weekends even if it might be shovelling coal or clearing out the hold with a only a distant prospect of a trip as a reward.

In naval days the VIC had a crew of 6 but we were amateurs with wildly varying degrees of useful knowledge, often needing to compensate in numbers what a fully skilled crew could do with far fewer. We were inspired by seeing what other preservation projects could do and studied nautical textbooks debating the contents and sometimes trying them out in a low risk setting. Not all the volunteer initiatives worked out. A visit to a naval establishment produced a generous proposal for some engineering trainees to come and help with maintenance. However the party never arrived, seemingly having "lost their way" in London's West End.

Over time the younger volunteers either became very committed or fell away as jobs, family etc changed their direction. *VIC 56* started to carry small people, born into holidays afloat, learning to row and even holding a children's party or two on board. They coped remarkably well and became valued crew.

Ship's Boat – an essential extra. Having a boat which could be launched when at anchor not only enabled a trip to the pub in the evening but allowed safe practice for junior rowers in sheltered waters, often, for example, in Stangate Creek in the Medway. Much of this was the doing of Edward Sargent who borrowed the boat to enter annually in the Great River Race. It rowed very well and notched up 14 entries. Since there were few places to go alongside in the Thames Estuary many trips brought the VIC to an anchorage and a means of getting ashore was essential. Edward Sargent, and later Mike Willis, became masters of the Seagull outboard to propel the vital link. Alan Riddell recalls "a memorable trip in the Vic's boat from remote Stangate Creek to the pub at Queenborough, where a boy standing up to his waist in water took care of the boat's mooring line for a small fee while you were in the pub. On the way back a thunderstorm came over, the sea became quite choppy, and it was quite exciting spotting and finding the dimly lit VIC by the light of the thunderflashes."

Small boat service in Stangate Creek (Henry Cleary)

Alan Riddell recalls some early trips on the VIC: "Barbara and I weren't involved in the original voyage of *VIC 56* from Rosyth to London, but we did get to know her soon after. We had several short trips on the Thames and one or two more unusual ones stand out. I often used to steer. I remember a journey from Ipswich round to London when I carelessly cut the corner a little coming round towards Felixstowe and VIC came slowly to a halt on the mud on a falling tide. It was embarrassing sitting there for several hours listening to the amused radio traffic between passing tugs and cargo ships about the 'funny little steamship sitting on the mud'!

Those were VIC's early days when the fire bars were inadequate, and a bit later off Clacton I remember some exasperated exchanges with Henry over his determination not to use too much coal despite the fact that we were steaming against the tide and making no progress at all towards a buoy a few hundred yards ahead. Because of these delays we ran sufficiently late that we had to spend Sunday night off Mersea, and spent some time negotiating for a passing boat to take Barbara ashore to some remote Essex railway station as she had to be back at work on Monday morning. The rest of us spent Monday night on the small ships anchorage off Southend. It was slightly choppy, and very dark and quite cold, with only an oil lamp, and I remember looking across wistfully at the bright lights of Southend Promenade and amusements and imagining sitting in a lively pub with a pint!

In the early days of *VIC 56* our older daughter was a toddler and our younger one barely that. They loved the VIC and we still have photos of them clambering around the boat, getting blacker and blacker, and one in particular of a baby covered in coal dust having it washed off in an enamel basin on the hatch cover with water which was as black as she was!

Upriver I also recollect when Henry had arranged to berth VIC in South Dock Marina at Rotherhithe and asked me to steer her in. The river was flowing reasonably strongly and it was quite tricky steering the underpowered VIC across the current and slightly sideways to hit the entrance bang on! I got the bow in with a bit of a bump and jarred the port side a little as the current pushed the stern sideways until she was entirely off the river. It was only then that Henry told me that there was only 9 inches clearance (or maybe less) on each side!"

Vic leaving Chatham in 2010 (Alan Jenner)

After arrival at Harwich – Bob, Alan, Rina, Denis, Richard, Wolfgang and Cleary family (Henry Cleary)

Skilled people with a more developed interest got involved over time. Backgrounds as varied as the Clyde passenger steamers, the National Maritime Museum and the Docklands History Group generated more talented crew enabling the VIC to go to places not attempted before. On one memorable voyage to Great Yarmouth the VIC was brought in by Iain Dewar, a Scottish helmsman adhering strictly to the pilot book, but on a heading that appeared to be destined to run aground (with the other crew standing on the focsle head apparently ready to abandon ship); of course Iain accomplished the entrance smoothly and exactly as the pilot book recommended.

Liz Cleary recalls having the family on board. "Picture the scene on *VIC 56* tied up one summer morning in mid 1980s, one small child being carried round the boat, up and down steps, by a tired mother, while the baby in his carrycot protested it was time to be fed, and nappies and babygros fluttered on the washing line strung up between the wheelhouse and the derrick. This was probably not the image the skipper wished to project, but we wanted to play a part in the action.

You might think that owning a puffer and having a young family don't mix well. There are questions to consider: in particular how much time are you going to devote to each? But in our case the boat provided distinct plus points, including opportunities for adventure, a chance to meet a wide range of people, holidays with a difference and a talking point with friends (which can be relished or viewed as something too odd to be mentioned). The adventures included simply being at sea, sleeping in a bunk in a cabin, arriving at a new place by sea rather than from the land, climbing the mast... Crew members were always willing to help entertain the children, whether by taking them sailing in our small dinghy (though the sight of a large sailing barge bearing down on her may have put one of our daughters off for life...) showing them how to row, reading stories during long passages or bringing an inflatable crocodile to accompany us. The visits to various festivals were also a chance when they were older to interact with the public, shaking the RNLI collecting tin or showing people round the boat.

There are some difficulties. Carrying small children up and down ladders is very tiring, and keeping them clean is almost impossible. There was always the worry that returning on the train from a visit to the boat I might be questioned by social services concerned that the children were being neglected. Baths were possible, but involved carrying a tin bath full of warm water up from the engine room.

Cooking on a coal fired stove is also a challenge, as well as choosing meals that all participants will eat, with ingredients which can be kept without a fridge. In the early days of running the VIC we had a rota for providing meals, and I remember quite a lot of competition (mostly between the women, it has to be said) to provide varied menus, including puddings cooked in the oven.

Another memory is of the voyages the family did not go on, either because there wasn't space for us, or because they were thought to be too challenging (e.g. the trip to Vlissingen). In those cases our role was often to meet the boat on its return and help to tie her up, standing on the quayside scanning the river to see who could get the first glimpse of either the VIC or the smoke from her funnel. With ship handling skills still in the development phase it was a service the skipper and crew really appreciated."

Trying to operate a vessel such as *VIC 56* means in practice having a "vessel manager" or suchlike who has the relationship with all who come to help. In the last century this meant evenings of telephone calls to see who might be available for what and how long, cajoling an offer, and then making this fit with tides and above all weather, which of course might have changed completely by the

Small children on hold at Faversham in 1984 (Henry Cleary)

A fried breakfast is coming using the galley coal stove (Henry Cleary)

date in prospect. Some friends would raise the game by bringing cakes, pies and a variety of enticing provisions but there was usually no fridge and very limited cooking possibilities.

Getting a good sense of what people regard as an enjoyable trip is the key to whether they will come again and keep the project going. Nor does that end on the trip itself; having decided whether the weather is good enough to go, you need to check how long people are happy to work in the engine-room, or in the wheelhouse, work shifts if necessary, and above all to watch the clock – if we need to go in 4 hours, that may mean you cleaning the fire in the boiler now. Above all ensure that there is always a boiling kettle on the galley stove. For the ship manager, the galley is often a good place for sensing how things are going and where help might be needed next.

Chapter 4

GOOD TRIPS AND SCRAPES

Trips were a way of incentivising VIC volunteers and fulfilling a purpose through display of the vessel to the public at Festivals in different ports. Planning them was an annual cycle; a list issued in January often proved wildly optimistic but having something to look forward to was part of the appeal. Over time limitations were better understood and we got better at judging weather, what was a good berth or anchorage, and the real feasibility of each plan. Even so incidents such as going aground were not unknown but fortunately the Thames Estuary is mostly sand or mud.

In August 1980 with the enthusiasm of new ownership, the VIC was steamed from Rotherhithe to Mistley on the Stour and from there to the River Deben, successfully managing the entrance sandbar. But the chosen anchorage proved a mistake with the anchor dragging and tangling with other moorings. The only resort was to hacksaw through the chain cable, buoy it, get steam up in a hurry and move further upriver; not so easy when the crew had reduced to 2 but fortunately a local off duty tug crewman came to our assistance. He later recovered the severed anchor and chain using a sailing club mooring lighter. This was typical of the free help given by professionals when there was a dire need.

The lower Thames, though hardly scenic, was rarely without interest in terms of shipping and seascape. Many trips were short– from London the tide allowed either a 2 hour out and back from the (drying) berth or 8 to 10 hours would get to just beyond Gravesend and back. Once or twice a year something bolder would be attempted, usually in summer visiting one of the small estuary ports such as Maldon or Colchester.

In 1984 we sailed to Faversham (where *VIC 56* was built). Even then the winding creek, steadily silting up, was only just hanging on to small coaster commercial traffic but we were keen to revisit and meet some of the retired Pollock's shipyard workers. A local coaster skipper, Heather Mitchell, was willing to provide pilotage and she steered the vessel expertly to a berth at the town quay.

The VIC has real limitations which have to be factored in to any planned passage. It is slow (4 or 5 knots through the water) which means not fighting a tide but dropping the anchor until it eases, and selecting a suitable anchorage. She is hugely affected by wind being light (in ballast), having a high bow mostly out of the water, and is

KEEPING A PUFFER AFLOAT

Vic 56 returned to Faversham, her place of construction, in 1984 (Henry Cleary)

Heather Mitchell, a local coaster skipper, who acted as pilot for Faversham (Henry Cleary)

underpowered for her size, a relief in one way since that keeps the fuel bill down. When meeting a fleet of yachts or small craft in a race, speed was dropped to the absolute minimum while these athletes were able to choose their own way past.

Vessel on Fire? – Mike Willis 2 July 1998 "I had spent that day in the engine room as we headed down to anchor on the East Swale for the night. Next day we steamed along the North Kent coast for the 80 mile voyage to Ramsgate. I was joined by Iain Dewar in the wheelhouse. The weather was fine with a calm sea and the rhythm of the engine gently clacking away below us contributed to a calm relaxed atmosphere. This was suddenly interrupted by H.M. Coastguard Herne Bay calling on the radio requesting information on reports of a vessel on fire off Whitstable. We realised that with no other vessels nearby, with our location and some black smoke rolling back from our funnel, it seemed highly probable that we were the 'fire' in question. We responded to explain we were emitting smoke – being a steamship. There was what appeared to be a brief stunned silence. We were then asked to steam in a circle so that we could be positively identified. Our response was that as we cleared the large number of lobster plots we were steaming through, we would comply. We later received a pleasant call of thanks. This was my Baptism of Fire."

Across the North Sea In the world of seagoing steam, Holland is a place to look up to; they do preservation well and it can be a real inspiration. In July 1989 we felt the Vic machinery – mechanical and human – was pretty good and decided to attempt a North Sea crossing. Navigation, using only dead reckoning (no electronics other than the VHF radio) and a towed log, was masterminded by Peter Erskine, an experienced yachtsman, one of a crew of 6, at times struggling to keep the vessel on course in the North Sea swell. Relay shifts in the engine room kept the engine revs up although the heat of a 16 hour crossing from Margate Roads anchorage to Vlissingen was illustrated by all the paint burning from the funnel. Dutch seafarers gave a warm if incredulous welcome, including Leo, skipper of a 1,000 tonne Rhine barge who put his back into shifting the VIC by rope while singing the song of the Volga Boatmen. Then we had to do it all again on the return one week later.

Alan Riddell, who came on the outward voyage, recalls "Rotherhithe to Flushing (Vlissingen) was a two day voyage, with the first night spent anchored off Margate. Crossing the Channel was quite exciting, not because of the grey weather, but because of the apprehension of crossing the separation lanes which all east-west and west-east ships have to use, without radar and at 5 knots. Without modern technology like smartphones or indeed electricity (though we had a battery to power the radio) we were navigating strictly by chart and compass! In the event there were no near misses, though the Hovercraft which in those days operated from Ramsgate to Belgium came for a whizz round us, and it was quite an experience to sight and pass the manned lightship (very different looking from

UK lightships) which the Belgians still maintained at the mouth of the Scheldt."

Peter Erskine, who masterminded the navigation for the trip, looks back "It was a trip only rendered sensible by the extraordinary reliability of the engineers and their charge, benign leadership and the ability to stay on the right side of the bureaucracy, plus of course luck with the weather."

From the start the London availability of the VIC led to invites to take part in special events such as the Royal opening of the Thames Barrier 1984 or the completion of Tower Bridge restoration and sometimes these brought money for coal. There were few working historic vessels on the lower river other than Thames sailing barges, the steam tug *Portwey* and ourselves. We had a network of sorts to exchange experience on our mutual challenges. One of the most successful of all steam vessels over these years was the paddle steamer *Kingswear Castle*, based at Chatham, whose skipper and business manager, John Megoran, readily advised and occasionally provided his talents as skipper.

Getting to a Festival was one thing but what could we offer once there? Moored alongside a quay we could have the public on board at "In Steam" Open Days and Festivals, looking round, including the engine room, and getting an idea of what it was all about. The heat and smell or handling a lump of coal and the basic 1940s interiors usually made more impact than any detailed explanation. With more planning we could use the steam windlass and

Going to Holland: Howard, one of the engineers, stands by the Walker log mounted on the stern which indicated distance travelled through the water (Henry Cleary)

Berthed in Vlissingen (Flushing), the Funnel paintwork having suffered (Henry Cleary)

Appearing at the Boat Show with steam tugs Portwey and Challenge, 2005

derrick to do a loading demonstration, or transfer coal from another vessel, as at Chatham and at events in the London Docks.

One frequent destination was the Harwich Sea Festival in aid of the RNLI which had a range of extra attractions including simulated lifeboat and helicopter rescues but these were eclipsed by a finale in which a daring motorcyclist would race up and down a cleared Halfpenny Pier (with the VIC a vantage point) before riding off the end in a leap of death into the harbour, leaving the motorbike to be recovered at a later date.

Coal loading with steam windlass at Harwich (Richard Beet)

Ready for visitors at Harwich Sea Festival in aid of RNLI – a regular summer destination (Richard Beet)

In later years the VIC attracted the support of two highly experienced working Thames skippers, Richard Beet and the late Alan Jenner, and this transformed the range of operations that could be undertaken, not only in terms of extending the cruising range but enabling us to take part in spectacular events such as *1541 A Ship's Opera* (by artists Zatorski and Zatorski) which meant holding station in a close procession of difficult to manoeuvre vessels for a spectacular light and sound event around Tower Bridge, watched by thousands. Another professional touch was improving the steering. Though tolerable if there was something to see and steer for, a trip to Maldon in poor visibility showed the difficulty in following a compass course. Richard Beet together with Bob managed to free the bottle screws and rod and chain gear and remove a chain link either side, so tightening up and this made all the difference. Generally Richard thought she steered well.

VIC instructed by Air Traffic Control In 2005 the VIC was invited to attend the London Boat Show in the Royal Victoria Dock, by the Excel Exhibition Centre, as described by **Mike Willis**. "At the Dock entrance a number of other vessels joined us ranging from a canal barge to an immaculate new white motor yacht alongside us, that matched us for length. Their white uniformed crew paid us a brief visit, but in my engine room clothes the invitation was not reciprocated! Ahead of us was the vast King George V Dock. With a sharp turn to starboard we headed through the Royal Albert and finally the Royal Victoria Dock - a 2 mile journey. At our berth, we were open to visitors until the Boat Show closed on 16 January, close to the public entrance and in company with coal fired steam tug Portwey and oil fired (formerly coal fired) tug Challenge, a Dunkirk Little Ship, and we had various volunteers staying on board during the stay.

Departure was on 17 January with John Megoran (of Kingswear Castle fame) and Richard Beet on the bridge. I was Engineer for the day assisted by Dan Cotgrave. A large number of vessels departed at the same time to meet a tight timeslot at the Lock. At the end of the Royal Albert Dock we turn to starboard across the end of the London City Airport runway. Large steel vessels at this point play havoc with the aircraft approach systems so flights were halted for a set period. The result of this melee juggling for position meant frequent instructions on the Bridge to Engine Room telegraph that ranged from Full head to Slow Astern. Richard said afterwards that he had never had to send so many instructions in such a small space of time. Once all were in the lock it was noted that an incoming airliner aborted to go around again. What a day!"

Harwich Sea Festival (Richard Beet)

Good trips and scrapes

Not all trips went to plan. Returning from Harwich one year a south westerly freshening to near gale off the Maplin left the VIC barely able to progress for a time. After a long slog the Medway was reached with much thanks to Richard Seager, steam engineer from the Portwey (Alan Jenner)

A fine anchorage – the Swale at sunset (Henry Cleary)

Chapter 5

KEEPING UP THE REVS

A steamer only really comes to life when there is a fire in the boiler and the smell of warm lubricating oil breathes from the engine room; maintaining the VIC in steaming condition was the number one objective of the whole project. Fortunately this was easy to get across to people and thanks to the steam and enthusiast fraternity there were a succession of talented and devoted engineers who came forward and whose efforts meant that in every year from 1979 to 2019 the VIC was able to move under its own steam.

Bob Cooper, the VIC's longest serving Chief Engineer, recalls his introduction to steamboating on a trip with his father on the soon to be withdrawn Humber paddle steamer, *Lincoln Castle*. Bob was impressed at how quietly the vessel moved through the water and how, compared with a diesel powered craft, it did not vibrate annoyingly.

"Later on I enjoyed a weeks holiday on the *VIC 32* in Scotland. The following year the ship's engineer Paul Marshall and Nick suggested that I return bringing with me my 'Engine Indicator', an instrument for measuring engine performance (pressure versus piston travel) which I did and checked out first the high pressure cylinder, then the low pressure the following year.

In November 1984, I joined the Greater London Industrial Archaeology group on a trip from Rotherhithe in London to Gravesend on *VIC56*. Larger than the *VIC32*, the *VIC56* was just as it had been in its working days, and I found the coal stove keeping the foc's'le warm was most welcome on a chilly day. At the end of the trip I got chatting with the skipper and told him about my 'indicator' experience. The following year I heard nothing, so I decided to write to the skipper and was persuaded to join the VIC in a week's time to help bring it from a Tall Ships Race event at Chatham back to Rotherhithe. I was able only to help with the trip as far as the overnight anchorage in the Swale. I must have shown promise as I was invited back to join the VIC at the Hythe, Colchester for its return to Rotherhithe.

It was on this trip that I met for the first time the VICs chief/principal engineer Howard Bolton and on subsequent trips we spent many interesting hours taking indicator diagrams, then making some adjustments to the Low Pressure valve events to get the engine to run slightly more smoothly. Another consequence of knowing Howard was getting involved in the VIC's winter maintenance activities. This involves among other things draining the water out of the boiler and a rota of removing boiler fittings, valves etc to check that they are in good order. Often we would put in a day's work on Saturday but thanks to the hospitality of the skipper I would spend the night with his family. The first time I did this we had a rushed bite to eat then rushed out as Henry was booked to give a talk which gave me a good background as the history of the VIC once he had taken on its ownership. Also it enabled me to get to know Henry and family better."

Bob Cooper oiling round the engine before a trip (Bob Gwynne)

As *VIC 56* steamed south from Rosyth in 1979, refuelling brought an unexpected encounter with Middle East politics as Government controls on large oil purchases had to be negotiated in order to take on fuel in Grimsby, Wells and Yarmouth. Oil burning with air or steam atomisation (which had required careful instruction in Rosyth) had not only prolonged the VIC's naval career but enabled her to be sailed south by our crew with little experience. But cost and logistics meant that it was not sustainable. Fortunately the VIC's Cochran boiler, though fitted out for oil reflecting national shortages in 1945, had been designed for alternative fuels so alterations could be made.

After running for a couple of years with one of the two oil burners removed and a lash-up of steel bar resting on firebrick support, burning coal and occasionally wood, full scale conversion began with removal of all the firebrick

Coal firing door fitted on the old oil burner mounting (Henry Cleary)

View of grate from below. Bright spaces between firebars show a fire burning well (Richard Beet)

and the damper plates at the bottom of the boiler and the manufacture of new firebars to patterns made by engineers Dave Morphew and Howard Bolton. Coal was cheaper, easier to procure, and even though it involved more work, both firing and ashing out, it was more enjoyable. On one occasion, thanks to one engineer, we even got some free coal in exchange for display of banners "Coal – the fuel of the future"; not very likely to be seen today.

Other engineers and how they got involved
In the early years engineering was led by Dave Morphew, and Howard Bolton, whose daytime work was with London Underground and British Rail Engineering and in later years by Bob Cooper. Wolfgang Siegert, an experienced German steam enthusiast, wrote asking if we could offer him time to

qualify as a ship's engineer and proved a really valuable engineer on many summer trips. James Packer is one of the VIC's experienced engineers and whose day job is working with software for designing new electric motors. Mike Willis and Rupert Lodge had sailing and steam engineering experience, Rupert on the Leighton Buzzard Light Railway and Mike the Welshpool and Llanfair. Both Rupert and Mike gave a lot of time and support to the VIC and many others such as the late Ross Alderman and Richard Albanese have also helped as engineers.

Wolfgang Siegert oiling the link motion (Bob Gwynne)

On 1st January 1988, as had been regular practice in early years, a short New Year's Day trip was planned but an hour before departure a roar and great cloud of steam from the engine room announced a burst boiler tube; no trip that day and a need to keep pumping water into the boiler until the fire could be run down. Retubing a boiler is to be expected every so often and has been done 4 times (by contractors) in 1988, 2000, 2007 and 2017, on the last occasion by Colin Hatch and Sam Thompson who replaced half of the threaded stay tubes, an extremely demanding exercise.

Heavy work – Bob Cooper One of the major jobs periodically undertaken on the VIC is preparing the boiler so a contractor can fit a new set of 'fire tubes'. At the forward end of the boiler there is bolted on a heavy curved steel plate lined with firebricks on its interior, which is called the dryback. This needs to be lowered down to give access to the ends of the new tubes which need 'expanding'. Fortunately the VIC had a chain hoist given by a shipyard, and thankfully there is a substantial beam from which the hoist could be hung. The dryback was suspended from the chain hoist and once the loadchain was taut the dryback was unbolted, swung clear then then lowered down to give access to the ends of the new tubes which needed 'expanding'. The nightmare would have been to drop the dryback and cause severe damage. The 'expanding' was verified by filling the boiler completely with water then hydraulicaly pressurising it. Once the hydraulic test had been passed it was time to raise the dryback up again except this time it was necessary to twist it slightly to get it to fit snugly in place. This was done with the aid of a small lever-pull and the operation was done when the VIC was sitting on the mud at low tide so there was no chance of the dryback swinging about and bending any of the clamping studs.

Bob with chain hoist after dryback removed (Henry Cleary)

A volunteer team and private owner cannot replace items as a commercial enterprise might do, so setting priorities is essential. The independent Boiler Inspector looks at the boiler history, the annual work programme by engine room volunteers – taking valves and boiler mountings apart in rotation and renewing where necessary - and gives an assessment which guides what needs to be done. All the Inspectors have been a great help to keeping the VIC in operation.

Tubes out to enable replacement of half the stay tubes in 2017 (Henry Cleary)

Engineers relax after a heavy day (Bob Gwynne)

Coal is now facing a rapid decline but it should be possible to substitute wood or new waste fuels at least for short trips. One consequence may be less of the unglamorous tasks of removing soot and ash and cleaning. These did have an unexpected benefit; the resultant "mascara" effect on the persons involved often had the effect of guaranteeing some free adjoining seats when going home by train or tube afterwards.

Every old boat needs a friendly shipyard The reality of a wartime built vessel working way beyond its design life (even from a yard as good as Pollock's) is that repairs and favours are a continuous feature. Developing a good relationship with one or more shipyard owners is essential, particularly if they are willing to treat you as a "hospital job" ie able to do the work when it suits them.

At the start at Greenland Dock, Rotherhithe, in the old lock entrance was a small base for passenger boats including Paul Deverell's welding and ship repair business (which later grew to become Thames Craft Dry Docking at Blackwall Point, used by the VIC on several occasions). In 1984 a friendship with Dudley Moakes, owner of Dousts, a shipyard at Rochester on the Medway, enabled the VIC to be slipped and given some attention to thinning plates (as usual around the stern and bow) but also an opportunity to acquire vital gear as the yard was closing (to become housing) and we were, if not the last vessel, then the last steamer to use it. In particular we gained a steel stairway for the hold, a petrol driven welder (operated by Edward Sargent to undertake many deck and stanchion repairs on board) and a Seagull outboard for operation of the small boat.

The yard most often used was Acorn Shipyard, Rochester and Strood, managed by Malcolm Fisher who provided great support to the VIC over many years, including annealing of steam pipes, lowering the mast to rig a new forestay, and replacing a section of the funnel as well as repairs to the hull. Acorn's closure was a severe blow for heritage vessels as well as commercial ones. Fortunately, in the last few years work for GPS Marine Contractors, the major tug and lighterage firm based at Upnor on the Medway, has enabled a new drydock on the other side at Chatham (operated by Stick-mig Welding) to offer ship repair and other services. In 2019 work of the highest quality was carried out on the VIC by the Polish and East European welders of Stick-mig Welding.

Doust's shipyard Rochester with VIC 56 on the slip in 1984 (Henry Cleary)

Doubler plates being welded to bow ballast water tank at Thames Craft Dry Docking, Greenwich in 2018 (Henry Cleary)

Acorn Shipyard, Rochester, lowering new top section of funnel in 2010 (Alan Jenner)

Chapter 6

JACK OF ALL TRADES AND MASTER OF NONE

In the early years, a typical scene at Rotherhithe was the VIC coming in to tie up - at a snail's pace so as to minimise the chances of unwanted impact with the unforgiving steel and concrete quayside. Conscious of the potential impact of 150 tonnes of steel, caution was the watchword in any location. Any plan involving yachts or other small craft in a confined space was vetoed as high risk. It also reflected having only a small crew and so I had to learn how to do every job on board, even if badly. This approach of tackling every task, including ship handling, gave both reserve capacity but also a way of attracting those more skilled who might think "I could do that a bit better". Over time we were lucky to attract many such people.

Despite all the skilled help some difficult decisions

remain before a trip, particularly around weather; are conditions are suitable and are there sufficient victuals, coal etc and have permissions been obtained where needed? Going down to get steam up on a cold, wet night before a trip, the enterprise often seemed masochistic and foolhardy but on a steamer warmth can soon be had and the wakeful night is not wasted as it can call to mind forgotten things that could go wrong in time to take some remedial action. Casting off the next day with a full crew aboard usually gave a wonderful feeling of release and, with everyone working a rota of duty/off duty, usually a good opportunity to catch up on sleep.

The aim generally was not to attempt ventures beyond our ability and "keep something in reserve". Once or twice we were stretched to the limit, with mistakes we learned from, but we had no serious injuries or emergency call outs and I give thanks for our good fortune. As the years passed we became if not more competent at least more aware, even if all formal recognition of steam vessels and competence in operating them had disappeared. After lobbying the RYA on this point, one of their senior personnel, the late John Chittenden, a former deep sea master and distinguished ocean sailor, kindly came on an overnight trip to examine 3 of us for Yachtmaster and after a return leg on Peter Erskine's sailing yacht, we passed! As Alan Riddell commented this seemed to be as much to do with his amazement at what we were trying to do as conviction as to our nautical knowledge.

For any old vessel, keeping up with regulations is a continuing worry and concessions have to be made. Some preserved vessels questioned in detail the Merchant Shipping regulations without much result. More compelling in my view was the underlying hint from the Department surveyors of "Go away and keep out of trouble. If you have an accident we'll throw the book at you!"

Wheelhouse apprenticeship – Alan and Hugh (Bob Gwynne)

Later we got some endorsement of a different kind when in 1994, with help from Alan Riddell, John Gummer, then Secretary of State for the Environment, was persuaded to come on board *VIC 56* for a look round ahead of launching Heritage Afloat, now Maritime Heritage Trust, on the paddle steamer Waverley. In his subsequent speech the Secretary of State lauded the work done in particular by the volunteer engineers on VIC – amazed that anyone would take on the dark, primitive coal dust laden conditions in the engine room.

James Packer, *VIC 56* Engineer describes what it's like down below at the Whitstable Sounding Zatorski arts event "As with '1541 A Ship's Opera' in London, *VIC 56* and *VIC 96* were each equipped with 16 steam whistles (and horns) so an indescribable music could be played. We were to steam in company performing an intricate dance close to Whitstable harbour, all the while accompanied by the chorus of many whistle tones. Those in the wheelhouse have no direct control of the engine, and all their engine control is through the voice pipe and telegraph, giving the engineer their orders. Meanwhile, the engineer is down below, and other than the glimpses through the skylight and doors, has very little idea what is happening above. In many ways, this is surprisingly relaxing, with one task to focus on, and no opportunity to see or worry about what may be approaching, but all the while keeping everything ready for the next engine request. With most people's experience of engines being the noise of an internal combustion engine, the peace and rhythm of the steam engine at work may be a surprise. On the

VIC, things have their own pace, and all builds up into its own rhythm. Keeping an eye on the pressure, fire and water level becomes a steady routine, if done in tune with the timescales of the boiler. This time the whole thing was accompanied by the chorus of the whistles, while idly wondering how close we were to the harbour wall and the *VIC 96*. An extra was that because of the steam demand from the very many whistles, much more attention to pumping water into the boiler was needed. Unlike the very earliest 'puffers' and steam locomotives, the VIC normally operates a closed water cycle, with exhaust steam condensed and pumped back into the boiler. This doesn't apply if most of your steam is going into a musical chorus, so I had the added musical beat from the auxiliary pump running to top up the lost water!"

Whitstable Sounding whistle rig and orange smoke (Alan Jenner)

Whitstable Sounding with rockets – homage to JMW Turner
(Alan Jenner)

One dimension which gives hope for the future is the great resource of twentieth century nautical and steam manuals which give clear instruction and were the main textbooks used by the seagoing workforce. The Royal Navy manuals in particular were designed to work even for someone who really had no prior knowledge or experience. Combined with practical opportunities to learn across the steam heritage world and some environmentally improved fuels there is no reason why marine steam should not survive for many generations to come.

VIC 56 benefitted from the lucky combination of being a family vessel and attracting a cluster of friends and enthusiasts. Once or twice the idea of forming a Trust was considered but collective motivation is different to that of the individual and with costs of £6k a year on average (more if shipyard work was needed) it would have needed many more than the handful involved to make this add up. There was also a practical requirement of needing someone knowledgeable who could be relied on to drop what they were doing and attend the vessel immediately if there was an incident such as damage, ropes breaking, springing a leak etc; this was necessary on several occasions.

Chatham VIC volunteers' celebration for 40th Anniversary of preservation in 2018 (Richard Albanese)

Jack of all trades and master of none

In many ways running a historic vessel is no different to a historic building or other large historic artefact; you need to be open to ideas about how it could be used in a way which attracts interest and support, so as to be kept in working order. The main task of the owner (or owners) is to come up with a plan, find people to help on a basis that they find enjoyable, satisfying and repeatable, then be prepared to fill in the gaps, eg getting up steam or clearing out ash and soot after the trip so as to minimise the time you need to ask of a more expert volunteer. Maintaining and operating the VIC greatly enlarged our lives and the circles of people we met – it brought much pleasure. It is now for the teams in Portsmouth to create their own take and find what works for her next stage of life.

New home – with the Boathouse 4 collection of naval support craft in Portsmouth Historic Dockyard (Henry Cleary)

In the Swale (Henry Cleary)

MORE INFORMATION ON *VIC 56*

Built: James Pollock and Sons, Faversham, completed December 1945 to order of Ministry of War Transport, Yard no 1840; Official number 180809; surveyed and classed by Lloyds for coasting service and managed by James Hay and Sons, Glasgow; registry closed 1947 when transferred to Admiralty.

Dimensions: Length overall 85ft; beam 20ft; draught (light) 6ft 6ins; 146 gross registered tons; cargo capacity 120 tons.

Propulsion: Compound steam engine by Crabtree (Great Yarmouth) of 140 IHP – cylinders 10.5" + 22" x 14"; boiler by Cochran (Annan).

For further material including films by Bob Gwynne see also www.vic56.co.uk and on Facebook – Steamship VIC56.

Boathouse 4 and Portsmouth Naval Base Property Trust (home for *VIC 56* since 2019) https://www.boathouse4. org/ and https://www.facebook.com/Boathouse4/

CREW AND VOLUNTEERS

Among people who greatly helped to crew and keep *VIC 56* running 1978-2019 are:

Richard Albanese	Kevin Kiernan
Ross Alderman	David Little
John Allen	James Littlewood
Gay Bailey	Rupert, Cedric and Suzette Lodge
Richard Beet	Bill McLelland
Howard and Janice Bolton	John Megoran
Colin Bowles	Margaret McGinley
Aelmuire Cleary	Martin McKay
John Cleary	Dudley Moakes
Julian Cleary	David and Joyce Morphew
Cleary family (Rosendale)	James Packer
Bob and Julie Cooper	Lesley and Ann Packer
Daniel Cotgrave	Tony Pickering
Janet Cox	Rina Prentice
David Dean	Alan and Barbara Riddell
Iain and Helen Dewar	Alex Ritchie
Paul Deverell	Mike Roberts
David Dewing	John Robinson
Peter Duggan	Edward and Ann Sargent
Margaret Edwards	Jenny Segal
Peter Erskine	Wolfgang Siegert
Malcolm Fisher and Acorn	Martin Staniforth
Stuart Floyd	Aileen Stanton
Alan Frith	Denis Stonham
Randal Grey	John Taylor
Janet and Bernard Hales	Nigel and Pam Thomas
Chris Harris	Gavin and Matthew Watson
John Harris	Nick Walker of *VIC 32*
Frank Hazlehurst	Stephen Watsham

More information

John Hurdle	Phil Weeks
Steve Jackson	Mike and Roz Willis
Stephen Jenkins	Duncan and Christine Wright
Alan Jenner	Tom Young and Catherine Cleary
Chris Jones	Andrew Reen and all the boiler inspectors
The steam tug Kerne engineers	And many other steam engineers and friendly seafarers

VOYAGES & OPERATIONS 1979–2018

Year	Days steaming underway	Main places/areas visited
1979	14	Granton, Sunderland, Whitby, Grimsby, Wells, Gt Yarmouth, London
1980	17	Thames, Queenborough, Mistley, Bawdsey, the Swale
1981	15	Thames and estuary, R Colne
1982	12	Thames, Ipswich, Opening of Tower Bridge walkways
1983	1	Short trip on 1st Jan
1984	18	Opening of Thames Barrier, Doust's Rochester, Faversham, Maldon
1985	14	West India event, Chatham Festival, Swale, Colchester
1986	13	Chatham, Swale
1987	14	Estuary (for Yachtmaster exam), Swale
1988	2 (after retubing boiler)	Higham Bight
1989	11	Vlissingen, Netherlands, Swale
1990	8	Swale, SS Robin event, W India
1991	13	Southend, Osea Island, Chatham
1992	16	Gravesend, Chatham, Bradwell, Swale, South Dock, Rotherhithe

1993	16	Stangate Creek, Rochester (Cory's for coal), Gt Yarmouth
1994	13	Medway, Osea Island, Tilbury, Launch of Heritage Afloat
1995	12	Acorn Shipyard, Harwich, Tilbury for "Classic Ships"
1996	10	Whitstable, Osea Island, Harwich, Masthouse Terrace
1997	12	Tilbury, Erith, Swale, W India
1998	13	Ramsgate, Acorn Shipyard, Swale
1999	10	Harwich, Stangate, Gravesend
2000	7	Harwich, Gravesend
2001	4	Higham Bight, Stangate
2002	6	Chatham, Stangate, R Thames
2003	7	Swale, John Prescott trip
2004	6	Higham Bight, Keith Hill trip
2005	11	Boat Show at Excel, TCDD drydock, Greenhithe, Brightlingsea
2006	5	Medway, Harwich
2007	3	Medway
2008	4	Queenborough, Medway
2009	4	Stangate, Harwich
2010	5	Hermitage Community Moorings, Wapping, Harwich
2011	5	Acorn Shipyard, Hermitage CM
2012	7	QDJP Pool of London, Harwich
2013	7	Medway, Harwich, Hermitage for 1541 Ship's Opera
2014	7	Whitstable Sounding, Medway River Festival, Acorn blocks
2015	5	Medway, Swale, Gravesend
2016	5	Medway, Swale
2017	4	Gravesend, Medway
2018	7	Hermitage CM, TCDD Greenwich